Face to Face

CROCODILES

Q2AMedia

Created by Q2A Media
www.q2amedia.com
Text, design & illustrations Copyright © 2008 Q2AMedia

Editor Jessica Cohn
Publishing Director Chester Fisher
Creative Director Simmi Sikka
Art Director Joita Das
Senior Designer Ritu Chopra
Project Manager Hemant Sharma

Illustrators Subhash Vohra and Aadil A Siddiqui
Art Editor Akansha Srivastava
Picture Researcher Debabrata Sen

This edition © 2010 Scholastic Inc.

Scholastic and Tangerine Press and associated logos are trademarks and/or registered trademarks of Scholastic Inc.

Published by Tangerine Press, an imprint of Scholastic Inc., 557 Broadway; New York, NY 10012

Scholastic Canada Ltd.; Markham, Ontario

Scholastic Australia Pty. Ltd; Gosford NSW

Scholastic New Zealand Ltd.; Greenmount, Auckland

10 9 8 7 6 5 4 3 2 1

ISBN: 978-0-545-32067-2

Printed in Shenzhen, China

CROCODILES

Sally Morgan

tangerine
press

an imprint of

SCHOLASTIC

www.scholastic.com

Contents

Senses

Their super senses are aided by their adaptations, like the third eyelid that protects the eye when it is under water.

Crocodilian Talk

Some of the noises that crocs make are warnings, and other sounds help them find mates.

Life Cycle

See hatchlings break free from their eggs and learn to get by in the world.

Saving Alligators and Crocodiles

Identify the major threat to the worlds' crocodilians and what can and should be done about it.

Facts and Records

Data, record breakers, and fascinating facts.

Glossary

Index

Meet the Creatures

Alligators and crocodiles are amazing animals. With their huge heads, **armored** bodies, and long tails, they are like no other living creature.

An Australian saltwater crocodile displays its powerful jaws.

Feared predators

Alligators and crocodiles are master hunters, feared by other animals and people. These expert **predators** live in and near water, hunting the animals that come to the water to drink. Their powerful jaws can crush a turtle's shell or grip an antelope's body.

Living dinosaurs

Alligators and crocodiles are often called living **dinosaurs**. This is because they were living on Earth at the time of dinosaurs such as *Tyrannosaurus rex*. The dinosaurs died out about 65 million years ago, but the alligators and crocodiles survived. Their appearance has changed very little over time.

One of the largest crocodiles that ever lived was *Stomatosuchus*, which means "mouth crocodile." It lived 100 million years ago. This giant grew up to 39 feet (12 meters) long and weighed up to 11 tons (10 tonnes). Surprisingly, this enormous crocodile fed on tiny **plankton** in the water.

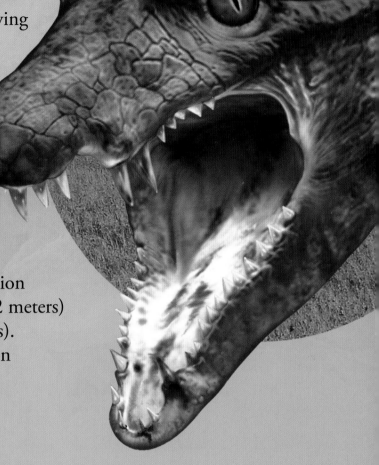

⊻ Alligators and crocodiles are found in the **tropical** and **subtropical** regions of the world, with large numbers in Central and South America and across Africa.

⊼ Montealtosuchus *was about 5 feet (1.6 m) long and lived 70 million years ago in South America. It was the link between prehistoric crocodiles and modern-day ones.*

Equator

area where alligators or crocodiles can be found

The snake is a legless reptile that slithers across the ground. Its scales are much smaller than those of the alligator.

Reptiles

Alligators and crocodiles belong to the group of **vertebrate** animals called **reptiles**. A vertebrate animal has a backbone. A reptile lays eggs and has a body covered in skin that has **scales**. Not all reptiles have four legs, but alligators and crocodiles do. Other reptiles include snakes, lizards, and turtles. Although alligators and crocodiles look like lizards, they are more closely related to dinosaurs and birds.

Crocodiles and alligators are close relatives of caimans and gharials. These animals are known collectively as **crocodilians**.

The turtle has a tough shell, made of two parts, which protects the body.

Cold-blooded

Crocodilians are **cold-blooded** animals. The word *cold-blooded* is a bit misleading, because reptiles usually feel warm to the touch. A reptile's body is unable to control its own temperature. Instead, a reptile controls its body temperature with its behavior. To warm up, reptiles bask in the sun. When they get too hot, they move into the shade. They are quite **sluggish** in the morning and evening, when it is cooler. Perhaps a better word to use is *ectothermic*, which means "getting heat from the outside."

FACT

The very first crocodiles were small, plant-eating reptiles that moved on two legs.

A male alligator reaches more than 13 feet (4 m) in length when fully grown. The skin is covered in scales.

Crocodilian Family

There are 23 **species** or types of crocodilians. They range in size from the African dwarf crocodile, which grows no longer than 6 feet (1.9 m), to the largest, the **saltwater** crocodile, which reaches 19.5 feet (6 m) in length or longer.

Three groups

Crocodilians are divided into three groups, according to how closely related they are to one another. These three groups are the alligators and caimans, the crocodiles, and the gharials.

▼ *The spectacled caiman is so-named because of the bridge of bone between the eyes, which looks like the bridge on a pair of spectacles, or eyeglasses.*

Alligators and caimans

Alligators and caimans live in and around **freshwater**, near rivers, streams, lakes, and other wetlands. Most of the creatures are found in North and South America. There are eight species of alligators and caimans, including two species of alligator—the American and Chinese alligators. There are six species of caimans: the common or spectacled, black, Jacaré, broad-snouted, smooth-fronted, and dwarf caimans.

Alligators and caimans are very similar. Both have a broad **snout** that ends in a rounded tip. However, the shape of the head is slightly different. The caiman has a more pointed head, especially the spectacled caiman. Also, the tail of a caiman is shorter than that of an alligator.

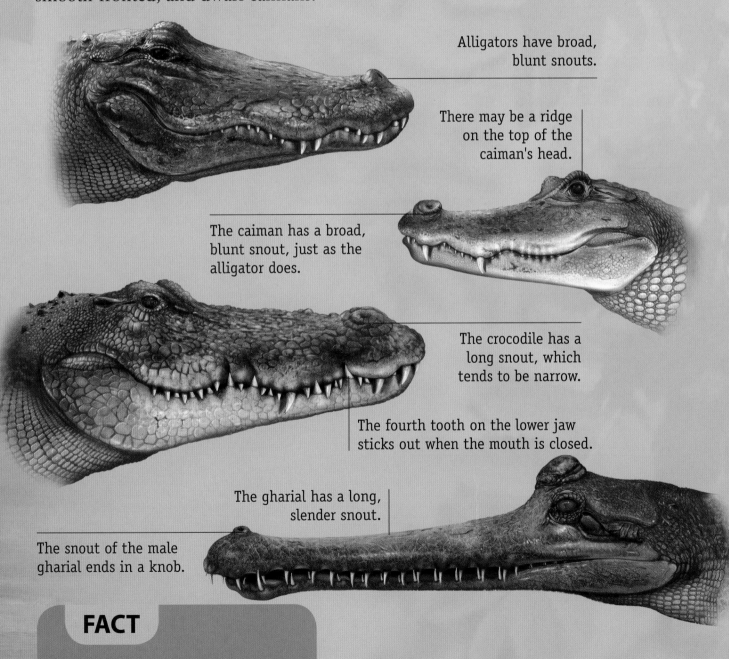

Alligators have broad, blunt snouts.

There may be a ridge on the top of the caiman's head.

The caiman has a broad, blunt snout, just as the alligator does.

The crocodile has a long snout, which tends to be narrow.

The fourth tooth on the lower jaw sticks out when the mouth is closed.

The gharial has a long, slender snout.

The snout of the male gharial ends in a knob.

The head of each of the four types of crocodilians is slightly different.

FACT

Caiman is a Spanish word for any crocodilian.

◀ The Orinoco crocodile has a long, narrow snout. This crocodile can grow 16 feet to 19.5 feet (5 m to 6 m) long.

Crocodiles

The word *crocodile* comes from an ancient Greek word that means "lizard of the river." Crocodiles are found in both freshwater and saltwater **habitats**. The shape of the snout ranges from short and broad to long and slender. There are 14 species of crocodile, including the American, Nile, saltwater, Siamese, and mugger crocodiles.

Gharials

There is just one species of gharial. The gharial grows 16 feet to 19.5 feet (5 m to 6 m) long. The male is a bit longer than the female. Gharials have a particularly long and slender snout, with many razor-sharp teeth. The snout gets longer and thinner with age. The knob at the end of the male gharial's snout is called a ghara, which means "pot." The males use the ghara to produce buzzing and popping sounds to attract females.

The ghara, or "pot," is at the end of the snout.

FACT

It can be difficult to tell alligators and crocodiles apart. Their color and general appearance are similar. The snout of the alligator is broader and blunter than a crocodile's, however. On a crocodile, the fourth tooth on the lower jaw sticks out when the mouth is closed.

⬛ Gharials are fish-eating animals found in India, Nepal, and Pakistan.

Watery Homes

Crocodilians love warm places where there is mud and water. They are found lazing on the banks of rivers and lakes and even along some beaches.

> ⌃ *Alligators in the Florida Everglades climb out of the water in the morning to bask in the sun.*

Heat lovers

Alligators and crocodiles need warmth. They cannot survive in cold weather. This limits how far to the north and south of the Equator they can be found. Crocodilians are not found in Europe and Northern Asia.

American crocs

The American alligator and the American crocodile can both be found in Florida but not usually in the same place. American alligators prefer freshwater **swamps** and creeks, while the crocodile is found in the southern tip of Florida. Crocodiles like the salty water along the coast and around the islands.

⊼ *The spectacled caiman is found in lowland swamps and rivers across Central America and parts of South America.*

South American caimans

Caimans are found in nearly all types of wetlands, such as marshes, **mangroves**, swampy rainforests, lakes, and fast-flowing and slow-moving rivers. The caiman prefers freshwater, but some caimans live on the coast, where they live in brackish water (water with a bit of salt).

FACT

The American alligator can survive the cold better than any other species of crocodilian.

⊻ *The alligator's coloring allows it to blend in with its surroundings.*

▲ *This gharial is sometimes called the Indian gharial or the fish-eating crocodile.*

Saltwater living

Crocodiles and gharials can live in freshwater, but they manage well in saltwater, too. They get rid of any extra salt in their bodies by using special salt **glands** on their tongues. Alligators and caimans do not have these glands, so they live in fresh or brackish water.

The saltwater crocodile is found across Southeast Asia, from India to northern Australia. It is found along coasts, in mangrove swamps, in **estuaries**, and along rivers. The young are born and raised in freshwater, but as they get older they move out to the sea.

Along the Nile

Nile crocodiles occur across Africa, not just along the Nile River. They are found in lakes, rivers, freshwater swamps, and small waterholes. When the temperatures get too hot, they dig holes that shelter them from the sun.

Nile crocodiles were important to the ancient Egyptians. The people feared but also worshipped them. Crocodiles were kept in temples. Some of the richer people kept them as pets in their homes.

⊼ *Crocodiles have long lived along the Nile River in Africa. The ancient Egyptians had a god named Sobek, who had a crocodile head. They believed that Sobek created the Nile, which provided them with water.*

Body **Armor**

Alligators and crocodiles have a protective covering of scales. While fish scales are separate and can come off, reptile scales form a sheet.

Scutes

A crocodilian's underside has small scales and smooth skin. But bits of bone, called **scutes**, float beneath the skin on its back and on the top of its tail. This skin has a ridged appearance. Alligator scutes are square with a ridge in the middle. Those of the American crocodile are rounder and ridgeless. Scientists can use scute **fossils** to learn about crocodilians that lived long ago.

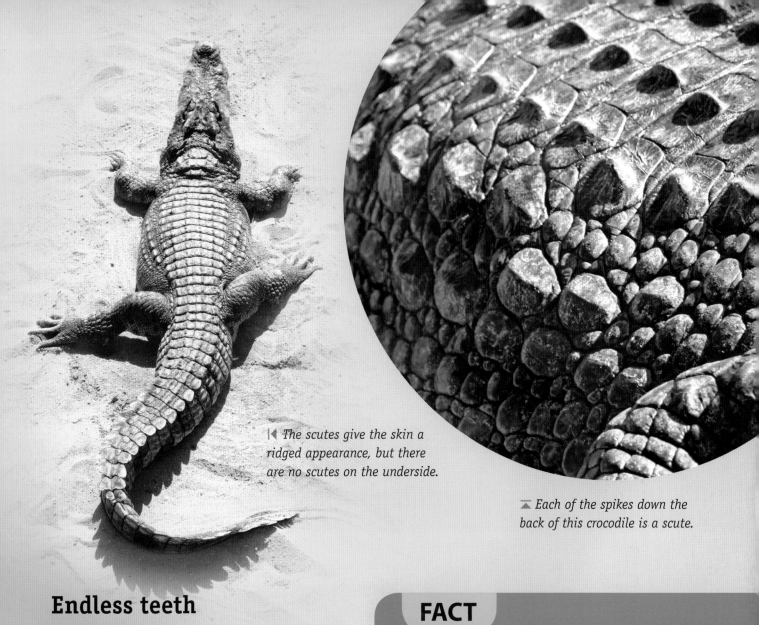

◄ *The scutes give the skin a ridged appearance, but there are no scutes on the underside.*

⏶ *Each of the spikes down the back of this crocodile is a scute.*

Endless teeth

Crocodilians have enormous jaws for their size. The jaws are hinged at the back, so that the mouth can open wide. There are about 40 cone-shaped teeth attached to each jaw. The teeth are replaced throughout the lifetime of the animal.

FACT

There is a suit of armor in the British Museum made from crocodile skin. It dates back to the third century A.D. and was probably worn by a priest.

▶ *The crocodile suit of armor in the British Museum.*

◄ *Teeth regularly drop out or break off when the animal feeds, so teeth may be replaced as many as three times in a year.*

Getting Around

Often people think of alligators and crocodiles as slow-moving animals. Think again!

⌃ The animals crawl up to 6 miles (10 km) per hour.

Belly crawl and "bunny hop"

Alligators and crocodiles usually move by crawling on their bellies. They go forward by pushing down and back with their legs. The smooth skin over their bellies helps them slip over sand and mud. They can go faster by raising their legs a little to give a bigger push. If threatened, crocodiles can travel up to 10.5 miles (17 kilometers) per hour. The back legs move forward at the same time. This movement looks like a "bunny hop." A large crocodilian is active for only a short time, however. Just 30 minutes of activity tire the animal out. It needs to rest for several hours after that.

High walks

Sometimes an alligator or a crocodile does a "high walk" across rough ground. It raises its body and part of its tail and positions its legs right under its body rather than to the side. It's hard work, so most alligators and crocodiles high walk only over short distances.

To high walk, the animals twist their feet so the feet point forward and not to the side.

To move faster while belly crawling, the creature raises its legs a bit.

Swimming

Alligators and crocodiles can look uncomfortable on land, but in water they are expert swimmers. They spend a lot of time in the water. Sometimes they just drift in the water, cooling down. At other times, they race after **prey**.

Their tails are half their length. The tail is flattened from side to side. It works like a giant paddle that helps the animals move through water. When crocodilians need to swim fast, they tuck their legs to their sides. This creates a smoother shape that slips easily through the water. Alligators and crocodiles use their legs to steer and brake in water, too.

Crocodiles have webbed feet that act as paddles, which help them brake and change position in the water.

Floating and sinking

When an alligator or a crocodile wants to float at the surface, it takes a large breath of air. The air in its lungs works like a balloon to help it float. The creature sticks out its legs to keep from rolling in the water. Just the head is at the surface. To dive, the animal breathes out and sinks.

⏶ *Most dives are between 10 and 20 minutes long, but some crocodilians spend several hours resting on the riverbed.*

FACT

When an alligator or a crocodile is swimming underwater, a large flap closes off the back of the throat. This flap is called the **palatal valve**. It stops water from entering the lungs or stomach. This means a crocodile or an alligator can open its mouth to catch prey and not swallow any water.

◁ *Sometimes, crocodilians sink downward and use their legs to walk over the river bottom or seabed.*

Danger in the Water

Crossing a river or coming to the water's edge to drink can be dangerous for other wildlife when alligators or crocodiles are around.

Lurking in the water

Alligators and crocodiles are very patient hunters. Often, they will float like logs in the water, with just the top of the head, the nostrils, and a bit of the back showing. They watch and wait. If they sense that prey is nearby, they sink and swim forward so they are within striking distance. Then, with a great push from their tails, they grab the animal in their powerful jaws. They pull the prey under the water so it drowns.

▼ *Waterholes are good hunting grounds, because animals come to the water to drink.*

Long and heavy tail propels the body through water.

Short legs

The prey is drowned in water.

Webbed feet

Strong, sharp teeth are frequently shed and replaced.

FACT

The muscles that close an alligator's jaw are very strong, but those that open the jaw are so weak that the jaws can be held shut by tape or a thick elastic band!

▲ A crocodile sinks its teeth into a zebra.

Leaping forward

Birds and insects sitting on branches above the water are not safe from crocodiles either. A crocodile can leap into the air and snatch them off their branches. To leap upward, the crocodile hangs downward in the water and then pushes upward, using its tail.

Strong bite

The bite of the alligator is one of the most powerful in the animal kingdom. The force with which an alligator bites down is twice that of a hyena or lion. It is five times greater than the bite of a great white shark and about 19 times more powerful than that of a pet dog.

This Nile crocodile has leapt forward to catch a wildebeest crossing a river in Kenya.

Crocodile

River crossings

Every year, herds of wildebeests cross the Mara River in Kenya. Crossing the river is incredibly dangerous. Not only are the riverbanks steep and the water fast flowing, but there are crocodiles in the water. Crocodiles wait to grab the helpless wildebeests as they struggle in the water. The young and sick are most at risk. Some of the wildebeests escape from the jaws of the crocodiles, but with horrible injuries.

Caimans are often seen lined up at the bottom of rapids, with their heads pointing upstream and their mouths slightly open, ready to catch fish.

A crocodile attacks a bird on a riverbank.

Trapping fish

Caimans and crocodiles use their tails to trap fish in the shallows. They swim about 3 feet (1 m) from the water's edge. When they sense that fish are swimming between them and the shore, they twist their tails and head toward land, trapping the prey.

Crocodiles work together to catch fish, too. They form a line to catch **shoals** of fish swimming downstream. Sometimes, the crocodiles remain in line, snapping at the fish in front of them. At other times, they herd the fish into the shallows, where they are easier to catch.

Croc **Food**

A hungry alligator, caiman, or crocodile will eat anything that moves, from snails and insects to birds, fish, and mammals. But gharials are fussy eaters and eat only fish or insects found in the water.

Swallowed whole

Crocodilians do not chew their food. Instead, they swallow small prey whole. They break larger prey into chunks. Often alligators and crocodiles toss their food around to get it into the right position. Then they throw back their heads and open their mouths so the food can slip down their throats.

Stomach acid

The stomachs of crocodilians are incredibly acidic. The acids help them **digest** large lumps of food. There are lots of stones in their stomachs, too. These stones act like teeth to grind the food.

▼ *The tongue is covered in taste buds that tell the animal quickly whether prey is good to eat.*

They sometimes slap
fish with their tails.

The slender snout slides
easily through the
water, like an oar.

Razor-sharp teeth are ideal
for gripping slippery fish.

Gharials are fish eaters that can
swipe their long snouts sideways in
water to catch fish.

Death rolls

If they catch a large animal, such as a gazelle or wildebeest,
they hold the animal in their jaws and shake it. Sometimes
an alligator or a crocodile will do a death roll. It jams the
prey under a fallen branch or other object and then twists
the body around, trying to break off pieces. Other times,
a second alligator or crocodile holds one end of a dead
animal while the first twists in the water to pull off pieces.

Rotting food

During the dry season, rivers and pools dry up and animals die from thirst. In the heat, the dead bodies start to rot. These rotting bodies smell disgusting to humans, but for crocodiles the smell means free food. They can detect it from hundreds of feet or meters away. The crocodiles often drag the bodies into water, where it is easier for them to pull the meat off. However, they have to compete with hyenas, lions, and other **scavengers** to get the meal.

A crocodile devours a dead fish.

Living on fat

Alligators and crocodiles move very slowly when not hunting so they do not have to eat every day. Typically, they eat about once a week. They lay down stores of fat in their tails. These fat stores allow them to survive for many months without eating. A large alligator may survive as long as a year without eating.

Every year, people are attacked and eaten by alligators and crocodiles. However, these attacks are usually the result of confusion. A person who is bent over and washing clothes in a river may look like an animal that is drinking water. Sometimes, people are attacked because a crocodilian is guarding a nest.

FACT

Senses

Alligators and crocodiles have incredible senses, which they use to find their prey.

Keen eyesight

Crocodilians have excellent eyesight. Their eyes are on the top of their heads, so they can see when they float in the water. They can see some colors, and they can see well at night. Their eyes are protected by a third eyelid, called the **nictitating membrane**. This eyelid is see-through. It closes across the eye when the animal is swimming.

△ *The pupil is an up-and-down slit which can open wide in dim light to let in a lot of light, helping the animal see in the dark.*

The snout is covered with sensory spots that can feel vibrations in the water.

FACT

One of the best ways to find an alligator or a crocodile at night is to use a flashlight. Their eyes look like round red balls in the light.

Hearing

Crocodilians do not have ear flaps on the sides of their heads. Instead there is a slit just behind the eyes, which leads to the inner ear. This slit is closed when the animal is underwater.

▼ *This is an African slender-snouted crocodile. It can detect tiny vibrations in the water caused by another animal's movements.*

Sensitive skin

These animals have tiny sensory spots in their skin that look like black freckles. The spots are found around the jaw in alligators and caimans, and all over the body of crocodiles. These spots can feel **vibrations** in the water. A crocodilian can sense when an animal is drinking water or when an animal is disturbing the water, such as when a fish is swimming close by.

Crocodilian Talk

Alligators and crocodiles are noisy reptiles. They can make as many as 20 different sounds, including bellows, roars, chirps, and squeaks. Each sound has a different meaning.

To bellow, an alligator throws back its head and partly opens its mouth.

Bellowing alligators

The Everglades in Florida can be an incredibly noisy place during the breeding season, when the sounds of bellowing alligators echo around the swamps. A bellow is a loud roaring sound, which is used to attract a mate and to tell other alligators to keep their distance. When one alligator starts to bellow, others join in. For about 10 minutes, there is a frenzy of bellowing. They also slap their heads on the water to make noise and bubbles.

Stay away

When an alligator or a crocodile is threatened, it coughs and hisses to warn other animals to stay away. If this does not work, it opens its mouth to show off its teeth, stands up, and flicks its tail.

Hatching calls

Young alligators and crocodiles start making peeping sounds when they are about to hatch out of the egg. These hatching sounds signal the parent to come and help them to get out of the nest.

FACT

The male gharial uses the pot at the end of his snout to make a popping sound and to blow bubbles, both of which make him more attractive to the female gharial.

35

Life Cycle

The life cycle of a crocodilian starts with an egg. The parent crocodile or alligator prepares a nest for the eggs.

Croc nests

After mating, the female lays her eggs in a nest and covers them with **vegetation** and soil. As the vegetation rots, it releases heat, which keeps the eggs warm. Alligator eggs are in the nest for about 60 days. Baby crocodiles take about 90 days to hatch.

▶| *The female crocodile digs out a spot in the mud for the eggs. After the eggs have been laid, she will cover them over with vegetation.*

The tail is used to clear the area.

The female uses her back legs to rake the mud.

When the young hatch, she will carry them to the water in her mouth.

To cover the eggs, she gathers vegetation with her jaws.

▶ *The baby alligator breaks the shell with its egg tooth and then pushes its way out.*

Get me out!

When young crocodiles or alligators are ready to hatch, they start peeping. These sounds tell the female to start digging so that the hatchlings can escape from the nest. The hatchlings break out of the egg using an egg tooth. The egg tooth is on the top of their snouts. This slices through the leathery shell so the hatchling can push itself out. The female picks up the young in her mouth and carries them to water.

△ *A group of young alligators from the same nest is called a pod.*

Predators

The females are very protective of their nests and attack any animal that approaches. However, they cannot stay by the nest all the time because they have to hunt. A nest full of eggs is an attractive prize, and many animals risk their lives to steal the eggs.

Living with mom

The young stay with the female for many months. She protects them from predators until they are large enough to survive on their own. Young crocodilians grow about 12 inches (30 centimeters) a year, but it is not until they are about 3 feet (1 m) long that they are safe from most predators. Their predators are monitor lizards, herons, snakes, turtles, and even other crocodiles or alligators.

△ *If there is plenty of food and warm weather, young alligators can grow between 8 in. and 12 in. (20 cm and 30 cm) in length in a year.*

▲ *The survival of young crocodiles is much higher if the mother guards them while they are small.*

Lifespan

Crocodilians that survive the early years tend to live a long life. Alligators live between 40 and 50 years in the wild, and crocodiles tend to live a bit longer. There are claims that some crocodiles have lived to more than 100 years of age, though none have been proved. One alligator lived to the age of 66 in an Australian zoo.

FACT

The females lay a lot of eggs because so few of the young survive. Only about a quarter of the eggs hatch because the others are eaten or die from flooding or disease. Of the young that do hatch, only two or three in every hundred reach adulthood.

▲ *A Nile crocodile gently holds her newly hatched baby.*

Saving Alligators and Crocodiles

Sadly, more than half of the world's alligators and crocodiles are at risk of becoming extinct. They have been hunted for their skin and their homes have been destroyed.

The Siamese crocodile has been hunted so much it has nearly disappeared. It is now classified as critically endangered.

FACT

During the 1950s, as many as 10 million Nile crocodiles were killed each year for their skin.

Hunted

People living near alligators and crocodiles fear them because the animals can be dangerous. Not surprisingly, many crocodilians have been killed so that people feel safer. However, many millions more have been killed for their valuable skin. The skin produces fine leather, which is made into shoes, bags, belts, and other fancy items. Nowadays, many countries have hunting bans and protect their crocodilians, but this does not stop **poaching,** especially in South America and Southeast Asia.

Habitat loss

Another reason for the decline in crocodilians is the loss of their habitats. Mangrove swamps along tropical coasts have been cleared, and marshes and swamps have been drained. Rainforests have been cut down, too. In addition, crocodilian rivers have been polluted with waste from farming and industry.

▲ *These caimans have been killed by poachers, and an official is throwing the bodies away.*

▶ *Shoppers are prepared to pay a lot of money for boots made from crocodile skin.*

Dead or alive

Nowadays, crocodilians can be worth more alive than dead. This is because many people want to see alligators and crocodiles in the wild! Each year, one million people visit the Florida Everglades, many hoping to get a look at an alligator or a crocodile. The money from tourism helps to save these reptiles.

▼ *Tourists look for saltwater crocodiles at Kakadu National Park in Australia.*

Saved!

The American alligator was nearly **extinct** because so many had been killed. Then the American government banned alligator hunting. Since the 1970s, the number of alligators in the wild has risen to almost one million. In addition, there are many millions more living on alligator farms.

FACT

The rarest crocodilians are the Philippines and Siamese crocodiles. They have tiny populations of barely 100 left in the wild. Both these crocodiles have been hunted and have suffered the loss of their habitat.

Around the world

A hunting ban saved the saltwater crocodile, too. Like the alligator, its numbers had fallen because its soft skin was in great demand. Action needed to be taken. During the 1970s, Australia was among the countries that banned crocodile hunting, and the number of crocodiles started to grow. Now, there are about 300,000 saltwater crocodiles in the wild.

▶ *This crocodile is being moved to a place where it will be safe from poachers.*

▶ *These alligators live together on a farm in Louisiana.*

Facts and Records

A The largest crocodile ever was named *Sarcosuchus imperator*. It is nicknamed Super Croc. It lived about 110 million years ago. Super Croc was 39 feet (12 m) long and eight times the weight of today's saltwater crocodiles.

The leg muscles of gharials are not strong enough to lift their bodies off the ground, so they crawl on their bellies. In the water, however, they are powerful swimmers, even in fast-flowing rivers.

Crocodiles do not have sweat glands. They keep cool by lying still and opening their mouths wide so heat can escape. Sometimes they pant like dogs.

When one crocodile shows its throat to another crocodile, this is a sign of peace or trust. An attack at the throat could be deadly.

Alligator comes from the Spanish words *el lagarto*, which mean "the lizard."

Gharials are sometimes called gavials. The second name may have started as a misspelling of *gharials*.

Gator holes are deep holes in the ground made by alligators. During dry months, water levels fall and swamps dry up, so the alligators make holes in the mud to collect water.

Over their lifetime, alligators or crocodiles may grow up to 3,000 teeth!

Stones, nails, glass, bottle caps, and other items that cannot be digested have been found in the stomachs of alligators.

Glossary

armored having a protective covering over the body, such as the scutes of a crocodile

cold-blooded having a body that grows warm or cold as the surroundings do

crocodilian general name given to crocodiles, alligators, caimans, and gharials.

digest to break down food in the gut

dinosaur large reptile that roamed Earth hundreds of millions of years ago

estuary a wide area where a river meets the sea

extinct no longer in existence, having died out

fossil remains or traces of remains from plants or animals long ago

freshwater water that is not salty; the type of water found in most rivers and lakes

gland an organ in the body that releases a particular substance; for example, the salivary glands in the mouth release saliva

habitat a particular place where an animal lives, such as a swamp

mangrove forested area along a tropical coast, where the trees grow in shallow, salty water

membrane a very thin layer of tissue

nictitating membrane fold of skin protecting the eye in some creatures

palatal valve part at the back of a croc's throat that closes to keep out water

plankton tiny, living plants or animals that float in water

poaching illegal hunting; for example, killing caimans for their skin

predator an animal that hunts others for food

prey an animal that is eaten by another living being

reptile cold-blooded vertebrates, which include alligators, turtles, snakes, and lizards

saltwater water that contains salt; the type of water that fills seas and oceans

scale a flap that grows from the outermost layer of skin, which becomes hard and, with other scales, forms a protective, waterproof covering

scavenger an animal that feeds on the dead remains of other animals

scute a flat, bony plate that lies under a scale

shoal a landform of sand or pebbles that is seen when tide is low

sluggish slow, lethargic

snout the nose or muzzle

species a particular type of animal group, such as the alligator

subtropical of or relating to the climate close to the Equator that is warm and yet has seasons

swamp a low-lying area of wetland with trees and pools of water

tropical of or relating to the climate close to the Equator that is warm and often wet

vegetation plant life

vertebrate an animal with a backbone, including fish, amphibians, reptiles, birds, and mammals

vibration a to-and-fro movement or shaking

Index